30 Days of Learı good deeds of Ramdan

Activity book

RAMADAN

Fasting chart

Color each star once you've completed the day of ramadan, you can do it!!

1 2 3 4 5

6 7 8 9 10

11 12 13 14 15

16 17 18 19 20

21 22 23 24 25

26 27 28 29 30

Good Deed Of The Day

Help in Preparing the iftar

About islam

"....so whenever guidance comes to you from Me, then whoever follows my guidance, then there will neither be any fear on them nor will they grieve."

Surah Baqarah - Ayat 38

About Ramdan / Eid

Ramadan is the ninth month of the Islamic calendar and is considered the holiest month in Islam

About our Prophet

Muhammad (peace be upon him) was an Arab religious and political leader who is considered the last prophet .
He was born in Mecca, Saudi Arabia in 570 CE and received his first revelation from Allah at the age of 40

Dua

O Allah, bring it over us with blessing and faith, and security and Islam. My Lord and your Lord is Allah.

Tirmidhi: 3451

I am grateful for ....
....

♥ ♥ ♥ ♥
♥ ♥ ♥ ♥

What are the
5 PILLARS
Of Islam?

The 5 pillars of Islam are 5 basic rules that Muslims must obey to live a good and successful life.

Color each pillar accordingly.

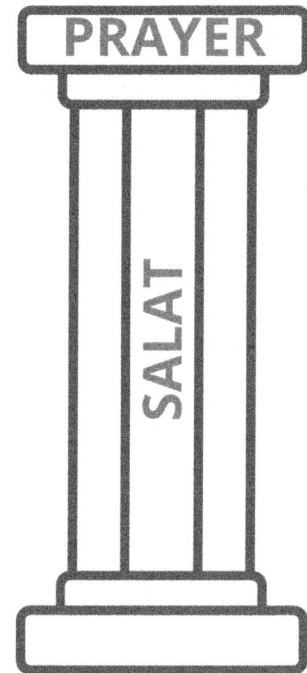

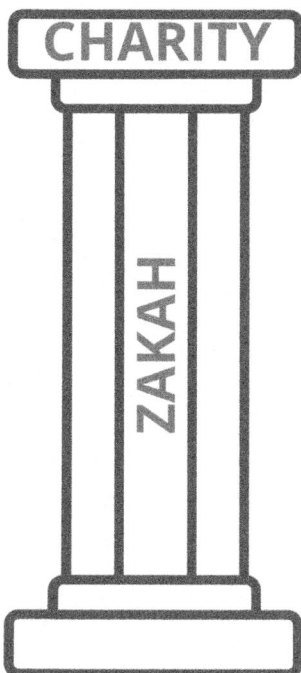

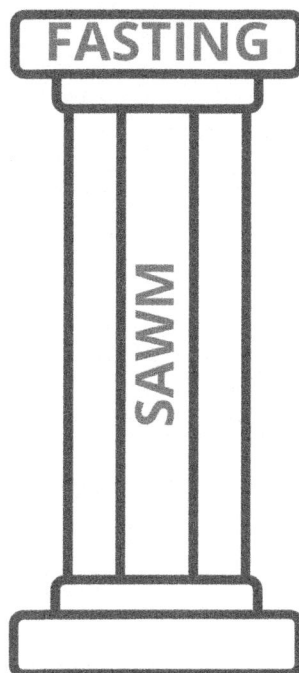

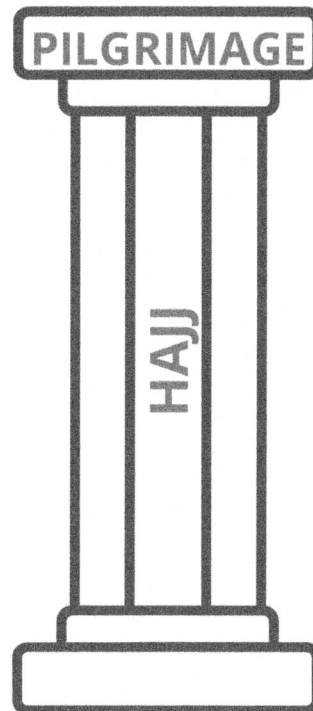

FAITH

SHAHADAH

PRAYER

SALAT

CHARITY

ZAKAH

FASTING

SAWM

PILGRIMAGE

HAJJ

Good Deed Of The Day

Smile at someone to make them happy

About islam

"Guide Us To The Straight Path"

— Surah Fatiha Ayat 6

About Ramdan / Eid

During Ramadan, Muslims observe a month-long fast from dawn to sunset, which includes abstaining from food , drink, smoking, and other physical needs.

About our Prophet

Muhammad (peace be upon him) spent the rest of his life spreading the teachings of Islam to the people of Arabia, establishing the first Muslim community in Medina,

Dua

Thirst is gone, the veins are moistened and the reward is certain if Allaah wills.

Abu Dawud: 2357

I am grateful for..
....

Who must FAST and who is excused

All muslims must fast during ramadan except for those who are excused from fasting.

Observe the given pictures and circle those that are excused from fasting

Traveling

Sleepy

Elderly

Pregnant

Small kids

Sick

Angry

SHAHADAH THE FIRST PILLAR OF ISLAM

The first pillar of Islam is the protestation of faith, also known as the Shahada. It's the attestation that there's no god but Allah, and that Muhammad (peace be upon him) is his messenger. The Shahada is the most significant aspect of Islam, and it's the foundation upon which the different pillars of Islam arebuilt.It's a simple statement that affirms a Muslim's belief in one God and the prophethood of Muhammad. The protestation of faith is recited daily by Muslims in their prayers, and it's also recited by those who are converting to Islam.

Good Deed Of The Day
DAY : 3

Learn and recite a new Surah from the Quran.

About islam

This is the Book about which there is no doubt, a guidance for those conscious of Allah

— Baqarah Ayat 2

About Ramdan / Eid

The purpose of the fast is to practice self-discipline, self-control, and devotion to Allah

About our Prophet

Muhammad (peace be upon him) is revered by Muslims as a messenger and servant of Allah and as a model of exemplary behavior. His teachings and actions are recorded in the holy book of Islam, the Quran.

Dua

O Allah! For You I have fasted and upon your provision, I have broken my fast.

Abu Dawud: 2358

I am grateful for ....
....

♥ ♥ ♥ ♥
♥ ♥ ♥ ♥

Act of Kindness
During RAMADAN

We should not only abstain from eating and drinking but also from bad habits or sins during Ramadan.

List down the good deeds that you do and bad deeds that you want to avoid.

Good Deeds	Bad Deeds

SALAH THE SECOND PILLAR OF ISLAM

The second pillar of Islam is Salah, which refers to the obligatory five quotidian prayers that Muslims offer to Allah. Salah is the most important form of worshipping in Islam, and it's a means of establishing a direct connection between the individual and Allah. The five quotidian prayers are Fajr, Dhuhr, Asr, Maghrib, and Isha. Muslims perform Salah facing the Kaaba in Mecca, which is regarded the holiest location in Islam. The performance of Salah requires corporal cleanliness, and Muslims must perform ablution before offering their prayers.

Good Deed Of The Day

Donate toys or clothes to a charity organization.

About islam

"....so whenever guidance comes to you from Me, then whoever follows my guidance, then there will neither be any fear on them nor will they grieve."

Baqarah Ayat 38

About Ramdan / Eid

Ramadan is also a time for increased prayer, charity, and acts of kindness. The end of Ramadan is marked by the celebration of Eid al-Fitr, a festival of breaking the fast.

About our Prophet

Prophet Muhammad (peace be upon him) is the greatest benefactor of humanity and a source of guidance for all mankind. Undoubtedly, the Prophet Mohammad is the biggest blessing of Allah bestowed upon man. It was Prophet Mohammad who bring people from darkness to light through his teaching.

Dua

Praise be to Allah Who has fed us and given us drink and made us Muslims.
Abu Dawud

I am grateful for...
....

Learn 30 Names of ALLAH

Learn a new name of Allah each day during Ramadan.
Color a new name each day and say it 3 times.

	MEANING
AR-RAHMAN	The Beneficent
AR-RAHEEM	The Merciful
AL-MALIK	The Eternal Lord
AL-QUDDUS	The Most Sacred
AS-SALAM	The Embodiment of Peace
AL-MU'MIN	The Infuser of Faith
AL-AZIZ	The Mighty One
AL-MUHAYMIN	The Preserver of Safety
AL-JABBAR	The Omnipotent One
AL-MUTAKABBIR	The Dominant One

ZAKAT THE THIRD PILLAR OF ISLAM

Which refers to the obligatory giving of a portion of one's wealth to those in need. It is considered a means of purifying one's wealth and a way to help those who are less fortunate. Muslims are required to give 2.5% of their annual savings and wealth above a certain threshold to eligible recipients, such as the poor, the needy, and those in debt. Zakat is often collected and distributed by Islamic organizations and charities, and it can be given in various forms, such as money, food, or clothing.

Good Deed Of The Day

Make a card for a friend or relative to wish them a blessed Ramadan.

About islam

"And do not mix the truth with falsehood or conceal the truth while you know [it]."

Baqarah Ayat 42

About Ramdan / Eid

There are exemptions. Travellers, elderly, sick, pregnant and breastfeeding mothers are exempt from fasting on the condition they make up missing days at a suitable time after Ramadan.

About our Prophet

The best way to express love for the Prophet Mohammad is to send peace and blessings upon him. Loving him, follow and obey him.

Dua

May the fasting (men) break their fast with you, and the pious eat your food, and the angels pray for blessing on you.

Ibn Majah: 1747

I am grateful for ....
....

Learn 30 Names of ALLAH

Mission 8: Learn a new name of Allah each day during Ramadan.
Color a new name each day and say it 3 times.

	MEANING
AL-KHAALIQ	The Creator
AL-BAARI	The Evolver
AL-MUSAWWIR	The Flawless Shaper
AL-GHAFFAAR	The Great Forgiver
AL-QAHHAAR	The All-Prevailing One
AL-WAHHAB	The Supreme Bestower
AR-RAZZAQ	The Total Provider
AL-FATTAH	The Supreme Solver
AL-ALIM	The All-Knowing One
AL-QAABID	The Restricting One

FASTING THE FOURTH PILLAR OF ISLAM

Fasting, or Sawm, is the fourth pillar of Islam. It refers to the routine of abstaining from food, drink, and other corporal requirements from dawn until sunset during the month of Ramadan. Fasting is regarded a means of cleansing the soul, developing self-control, and displaying solidarity with the poor and indigent. During the month of Ramadan, Muslims also engage in fresh acts of worshipping, similar as reading the Quran and making extra prayers. The end of Ramadan is labeled by a festivity called Eid al-Fitr, which is a time for Muslims to come together and celebrate their faith.

Good Deed Of The Day

Memorize the names of Allah.

About islam

"So remember Me; I will remember you. And be grateful to Me and do not deny Me."

Surah Baqarah Verse 152

About Ramdan / Eid

A fasting person physically feels the value of, and their need for, basic sustenance when they experience the pangs of hunger and thirst.

About our Prophet

Prophet Muhammad (peace be upon him) faced numerous challenges during his lifetime, including persecution and opposition from the Meccan elite.
He and his followers eventually migrated to Medina in 622 CE,which is known as the Hijra and marks the beginning of the Islamic calendar.

Dua

Oh Everliving, The Everlasting, I seek Your help through Your mercy.

I am grateful for..

....

Learn 30 Names of ALLAH

Mission 8: Learn a new name of Allah each day during Ramadan.
Color a new name each day and say it 3 times.

	MEANING
AL-BAASIT	The Extender
AL-KHAAFID	The Reducer
AR-RAFI	The Elevating One
AL-MU'IZZ	The Honourer-bestower
AL-MUZIL	The Abaser
AS-SAMI'	The All-Hearer
AL-BASEER	The All-Seeing
AL-HAKAM	The Impartial Judge
AL-ADL	The Embodiment of Justice
AL-LATEEF	The Knower of Subtleties

HADJ THE FIFTH PILLAR OF ISLAM

Hajj is the last pillar of Islam. It refers to the passage to the holy town of Mecca that all capable- bodied Muslims are needed to perform at least once in their life, handed they've the financial means to do so. The Hajj is a trip of spiritual signification, and it involves a number of practices that commemorate the Prophet Ibrahim's(Abraham's) devotion to Allah. Muslims who take over the pilgrimage wear simple white apparel to emblematize equality and harmony.

Good Deed Of The Day
DAY : 7

Donate toys or clothes to a charity organization.

About islam

"....so whenever guidance comes to you from Me, then whoever follows my guidance, then there will neither be any fear on them nor will they grieve."

Baqarah Ayat 38

About Ramdan / Eid

Muslims fasts for the sake of God, they acknowledge the sustenance, which may be taken for granted, actually comes from God. Therefore, fasting is the best way to show a true and sincere thanksgiving.

About our Prophet

Prophet Muhammad (peace be upon him) is the greatest benefactor of humanity and a source of guidance for all mankind. Undoubtedly, the Prophet Mohammad is the biggest blessing of Allah bestowed upon man. It was Prophet Mohammad who bring people from darkness to light through his teaching.

Dua

Praise be to Allah Who has fed us and given us drink and made us Muslims.
Abu Dawud

I am grateful for ....
....

ALPHABET Tracing

Let's trace the lowercase letters below!

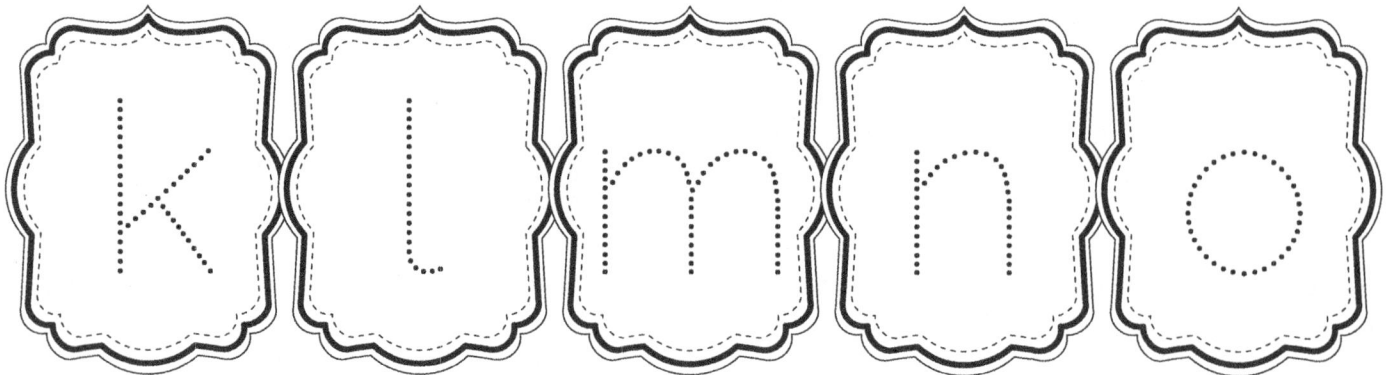

a b c d e

f g h i j

k l m n o

Good Deed Of The Day

Help clean up the local mosque.

About islam

"Indeed we belong to Allah, and indeed to Him we will return"

Ayat 156

About Ramdan / Eid

Ramadan is an ideal time to read and reflect on the Quran, Many Muslims aim to complete the entire Quran during Ramadan, and they may attend Taraweeh prayers at the mosque to listen to recitations of the Quran.

About our Prophet

Prophet Muhammad (peace be upon him) In Medina, had established the first Islamic community and worked to establish peace and justice among its members. He also led a number of battles against those who sought to harm the Muslim community.

Dua

I seek forgiveness from Allah for all my sins and turn to Him.

I am grateful for ....

....

ALPHABET Tracing

Let's trace the lowercase letters below!

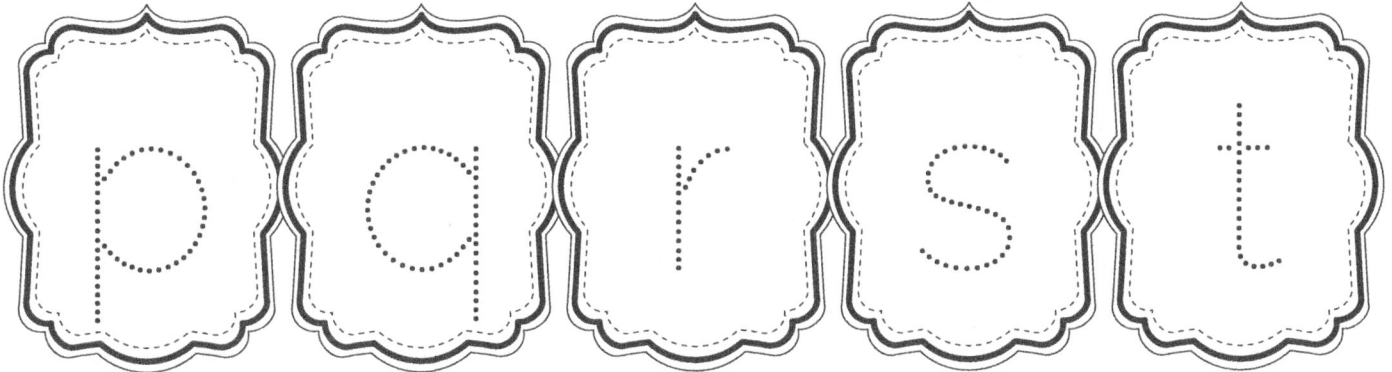

p q r s t

u v w x y

z

Surah Al fatiha the Opening

1. In the name of Allah, the Gracious, the Merciful.

2. Praise be to Allah, Lord of the Worlds.

3. The Most Gracious, the Most Merciful.

4. Master of the Day of Judgment.

5. It is You we worship, and upon You we call for help.

6. Guide us to the straight path.

7. The path of those You have blessed, not of those against whom there is anger, nor of those who are misguided.

Good Deed Of The Day

Learn about the history of Islam and Prophet Muhammad.

About islam

"And hold firmly to the rope of Allah all together and do not become divided."

Surah al imran -Ayat 103

About Ramdan / Eid

Through fasting, the rich know what it means to be hungry. Hence, the rich will be more inclined to give charity when they fast. The rich organise break-fast dinners (iftar) for the poor.

About our Prophet

Throughout his life, Prophet Muhammad emphasized the importance of compassion, mercy, and justice. He was known for his kindness and generosity, and he encouraged his followers to treat all people with respect and dignity..

Dua

None has the right to be worshipped except Allah, alone, without partner, to Him belongs all sovereignty and praise,He gives life and causes death and He is over all things omnipotent.

At-Tirmidhi 5:515

I am grateful for ....
....

NUMBER Tracing

Let's trace the numbers below!

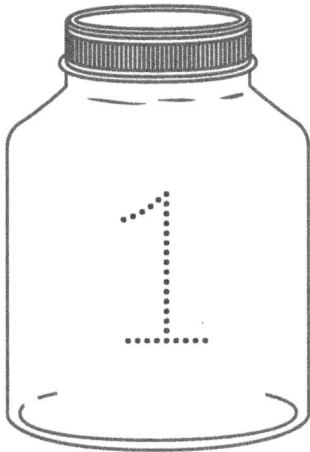

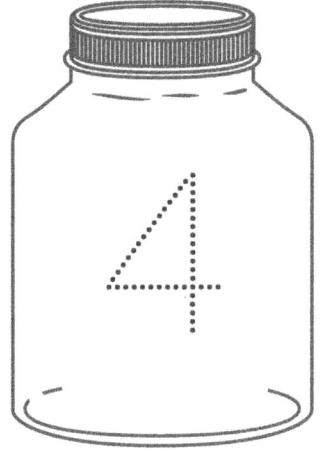

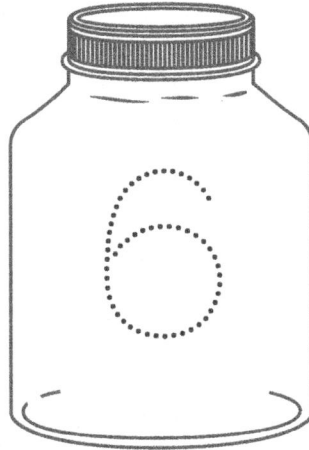

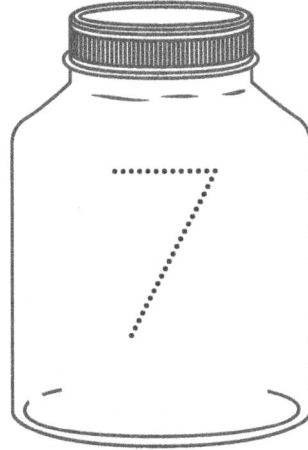

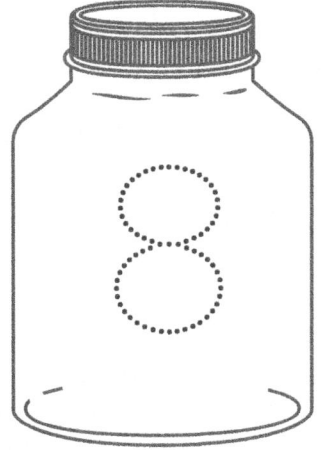

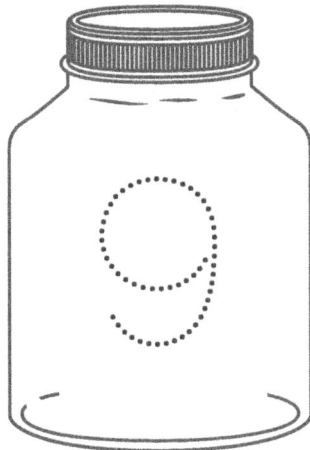

1   2   3   4

5   6   7   8

9   10

Surah Al Nas
Mankind

In the name of God, the Gracious, the Merciful.

1. Say, "I seek refuge in the Lord of mankind.

2. The King of mankind.

3. The God of mankind.

4. From the evil of the sneaky whisperer.

5. Who whispers into the hearts of people.

6. From among jinn and among people."

Good Deed Of The Day

Plant a seed on a garden.

About islam

"Your ally is none but Allah and [therefore] His Messenger and those who have believed — those who establish prayer and give zakah, and they bow [in worship]."
Surah al Maidah Verse 55

About Ramdan / Eid

In addition to the five daily prayers, Muslims may perform additional prayers during Ramadan, such as the Taraweeh prayers at night. These prayers are a means of increasing one's connection to Allah and seeking His forgiveness.

About our Prophet

Prophet Muhammad (peace be upon him) lived a humble life as a merchant and shepherd until he received his first revelation from Allah at the age of 40. He spent the rest of his life spreading the message of Islam and guiding his followers in the ways of Allah.

Dua

None has the right to be worshipped except Allah, alone, without partner, to Him belongs all sovereignty and praise, He gives life and causes death and He is over all things omnipotent.

At-Tirmidhi 5:515

I am grateful for..
....
♥ ♥ ♥ ♥
♥ ♥ ♥ ♥

Connect the dots

and color

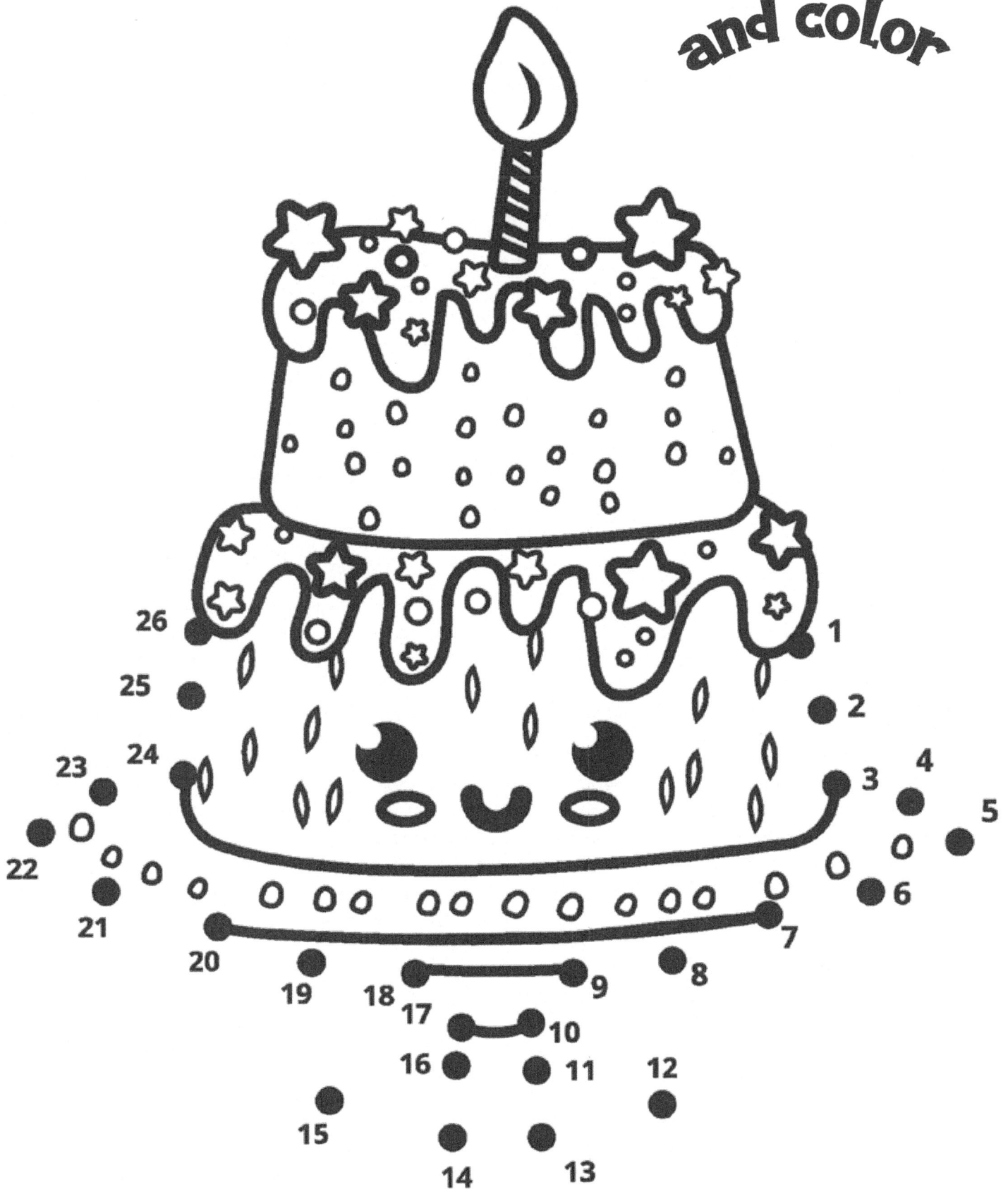

Surah AL-IKHLAS
Sincerity

In the name of God, the Gracious, the Merciful.

1 .Say, "He is Allah , [who is] One,

2 .Allah , the Eternal Refuge.

3 .He neither begets nor is born,

4 .Nor is there to Him any equivalent."

Good Deed Of The Day

Look after a neighbor's pet or help an elderly neighbor.

About islam

"Those who have gone astray will not harm you when you have been guided. To Allah is your return all together; then He will inform you of what you used to do."

Surah al maidah - Ayat 105

About Ramdan / Eid

Spending time with family and friends Ramadan is also a time for community and togetherness. Many Muslims spend time with family and friends during Ramadan, sharing meals and taking part in community events.

About our Prophet

Prophet Muhammad, peace be upon him, was known for his kindness and compassion towards all people, regardless of their background or circumstances. He treated everyone with respect and dignity, and he encouraged his followers to do the same.

Dua

O Allah, I ask You for knowledge which is beneficial and sustenance which is good, and deeds which are acceptable.

Ibn Majah 1:152

I am grateful for ....
....

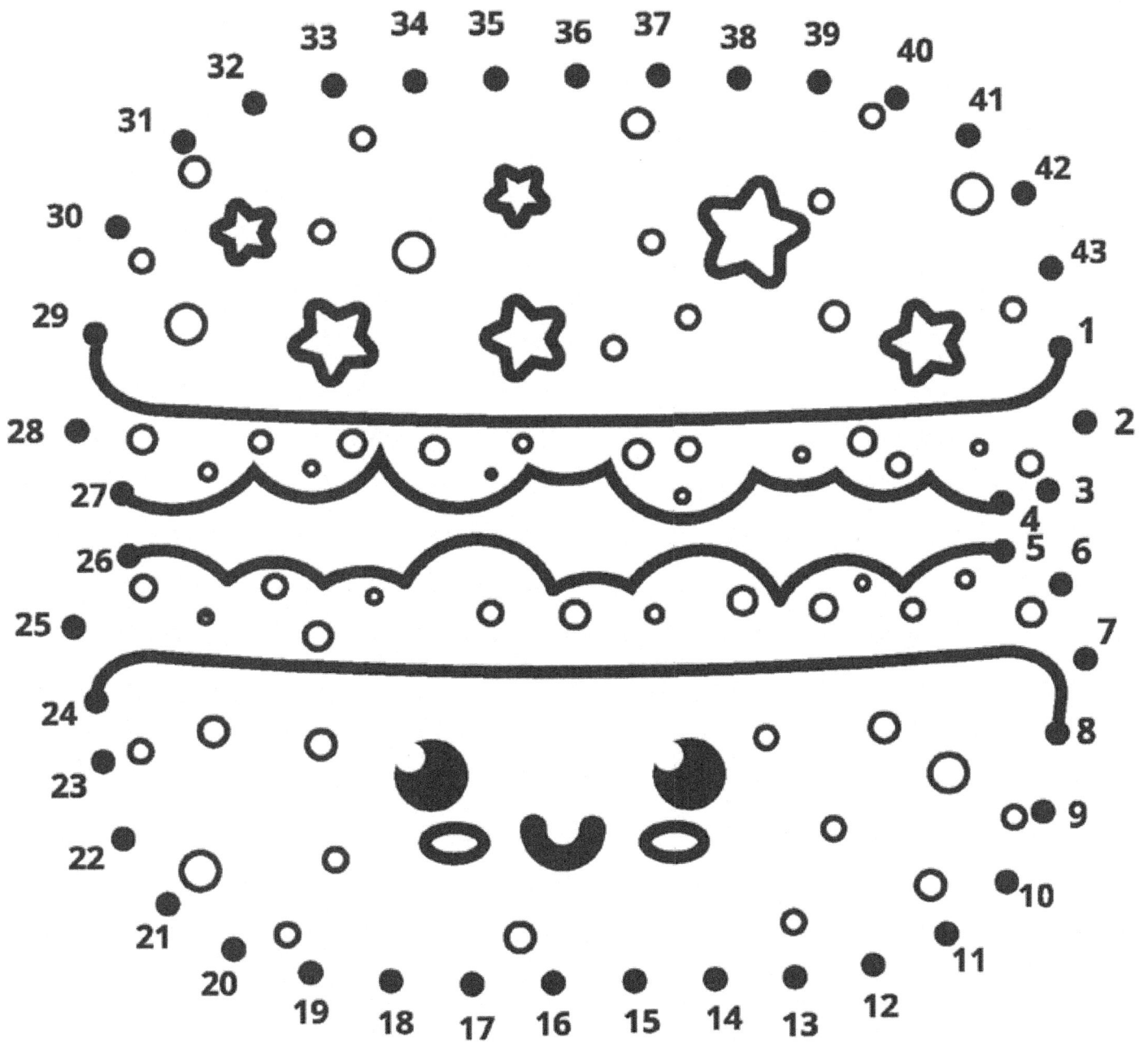

Connect the dots

and color

33 34 35 36 37 38 39 40
32 41
31 42
30 43
29 1
28 2
27 3
4
26 5 6
25 7
24 8
23 9
22 10
21 11
20 12
19 18 17 16 15 14 13

Surah Al falaq
Daybreak

In the name of Allah, the Gracious, the Merciful.

1 Say, "I seek refuge in the Lord of daybreak

2 From the evil of that which He created

3 And from the evil of darkness when it settles

4 And from the evil of the blowers in knots

5 And from the evil of an envier when he envies."

Good Deed Of The Day

Visit a sick relative or friend.

About islam

"And it is He who created the heavens and earth in truth. And the day He says, "Be," and it is, His word is the truth.

Surah al Anam -Ayat 73

About Ramdan / Eid

Ramadan is a time for Muslims to focus on their spiritual growth and to connect more deeply with Allah.

About our Prophet

Prophet Muhammad was particularly kind to the poor and needy, and he would often give generously to those in need, even if it meant sacrificing his own needs. He would visit the sick and offer words of comfort, and he would help those who were struggling in any way he could.

Dua

O Allah, I have greatly wronged myself and no one forgives sins but You. So, grant me forgiveness and have mercy on me. Surely, you are Forgiving, Merciful.

An-Nasa'i: 1303, Al-Bukhari: 834.

I am grateful for

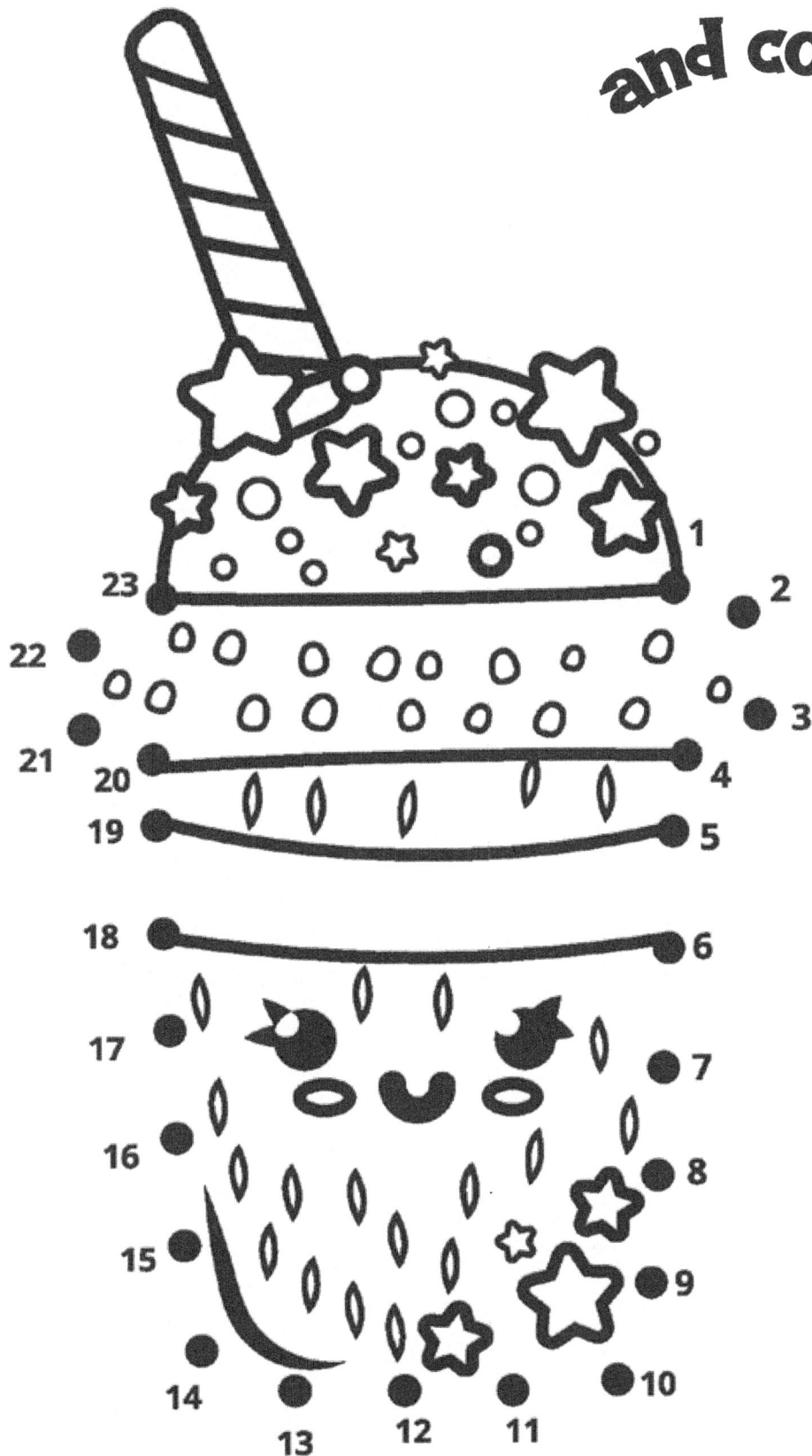

Connect the dots

and color

23 22 21 20 19 18 17 16 15 14 13 12 11 10 9 8 7 6 5 4 3 2 1

Surah Al kawtar Abundance

In the name of Allah, the Gracious, the Merciful.

1 Indeed, We have granted you, [O Muhammad], al-Kawthar.

2 So pray unto thy Lord, and sacrifice.

3 Indeed, your enemy is the one cut off.

Good Deed Of The Day

Attend Taraweeh prayers at the mosque.

About islam

"And the worldly life is not but amusement and diversion; but the home of the Hereafter is best for those who fear Allah, so will you not reason?"

Surah Anam Ayat 32

About Ramdan / Eid

Be optimistic towards life, specially towards Allah in particular and always expect good omen from Allah. Always ask Allah for His forgiveness rather than expecting His Anger and punishment.

About our Prophet

Prophet Muhammad was also known for his kindness towards children. He would play with them, tell them stories, and show them affection, setting an example for his followers to treat children with kindness and respect.

Dua

O Allah, forgive me what I have sent before me and what I have left behind me, what I have concealed and what I have done openly, what I have done in excess , and what You are better aware of than I . You are the One Who sends forth and You are the One Who delays .There is none worthy of worship but You.

Abu Dawud: 1509

I am grateful for ....
....

♥ ♥ ♥ ♥
♥ ♥ ♥ ♥

Connect the dots

and color

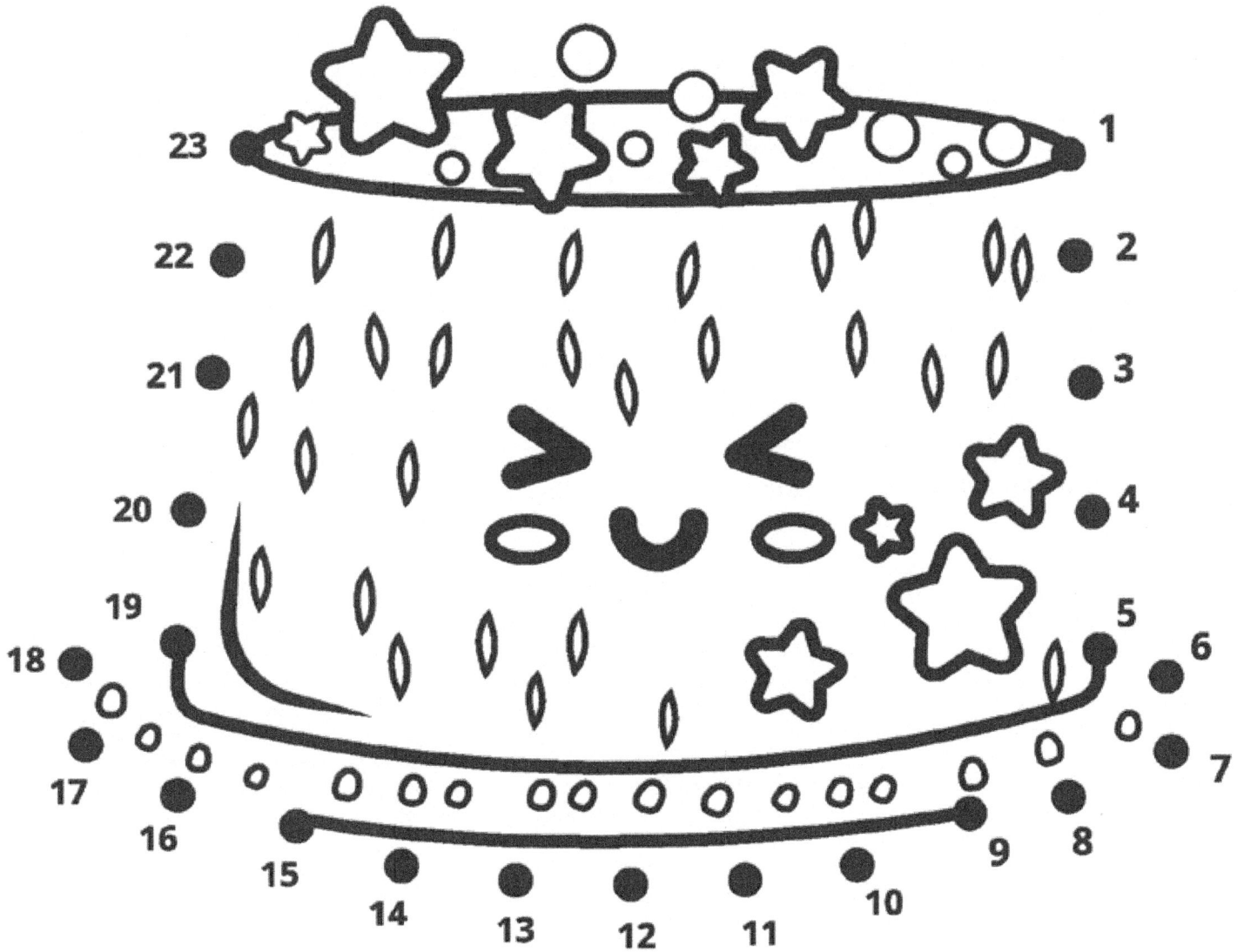

Surah Al nasr
Succour

In the name of Allah, the Gracious, the Merciful.

1 When the victory of Allah has come and the conquest,

2 And you see the people entering into the religion of Allah in multitudes,

3 Then exalt [Him] with praise of your Lord and ask forgiveness of Him. Indeed, He is ever Accepting of repentance.

Good Deed Of The Day

Volunteer at an Islamic event or fundraiser.

About islam

"Indeed, the mercy of Allah is near to the doers of good."

Surah Anam Ayah 56

About Ramdan / Eid

Fasting purifies the physical body from toxins, helps discipline the soul and purify it from the blameworthy

About our Prophet

The passing of Khadijah happened 10 years after the revelation. She was the Prophet Muhammed's beloved wife for 23 years. She was the first person to comfort Him after He received revelation. She was also the first person to accept Islam.

Dua

Glory is to You, O Allah, and praise is to You. I bear witness that there is none worthy of worship but You. I seek Your forgiveness and repent to You.

Abu Dawud: 4859

I am grateful for ....
....

find the way to the Nice cake its iftar time!

Good Deed Of The Day

Learn about a new Islamic country or culture

About islam

My mercy encompasses all things."
So I will decree it [especially] for those who fear Me and give zakah and those who believe in Our verses —"
Surah Al A'raf Ayat 156

About Ramdan / Eid

Fasting gives the digestive system a much-needed break, allowing the body to focus on other functions such as detoxification. This can lead to improved liver function, improved metabolism, and a strengthened immune system.

About our Prophet

Prophet Muhammad's kindness extended even to his enemies. Despite facing persecution and opposition from many quarters, he would often respond with patience, forgiveness, and kindness, seeking to win people over through his example.

Dua

O Allah, I seek refuge in you from grief and sadness, from weakness and from laziness, from miserliness and from cowardice, from being overcome by debt and overpowered by men (i .e . others).
Al-Bukhari: 2893

I am grateful for ....
....

The camel is trapped help him to get out!

Good Deed Of The Day

Help with the grocery shopping and cooking for iftar

About islam

"Take what is given freely, enjoin what is good, and turn away from the ignorant. And if an evil suggestion comes to you from Satan, then seek refuge in Allah . Indeed, He is Hearing and Knowing."

Surah Al-A'raf Ayat 199-200

About Ramdan / Eid

Fasting can lead to weight loss as the body burns stored fat for energy when it is not receiving food. However, it is important to maintain a healthy diet during non-fasting hours to ensure proper nutrition

About our Prophet

Victory at Battle of Badr On the 17th of Ramadan, in the second year of Hijra, the Prophet Muhammed and His companions went out to fight their first battle against the Meccans. The muslims at the time were significantly outnumbered by the enemy. Allah sent down angels to aid the believers during the battle. Thus resulting in victory.

Dua

All praise is for Allah, Who fed us and gave us drink, and Who is sufficient for us and has sheltered us, for how many have none to suffice them or shelter them.

Muslim 4: 2083

I am grateful for...
....

Help them get the chair

Good Deed Of The Day

Make a dua list for your family and friends

About islam

"So when the Qur'an is recited, then listen to it and pay attention that you may receive mercy."

surah al A'raf-Ayat 204

About Ramdan / Eid

have a good opinion of Allah and never be pessimistic or despair of his Mercy. Know that He will reward you for your deeds.
Hope is preferred over fear whilst both should be present.

About our Prophet

Victory at Battle of Badr
On the 17th of Ramadan, Abu Jahl, the enemy of the Prophet, died.

"Allah helped you at Badr when you were very weak. Be mindful of Allah, so that you may be grateful" (3:123)

Dua

Glory is to You, O Allah, our Lord, and praise is Yours. O Allah, forgive me.

Al-Bukhari: 794

I am grateful for ....
....

Find the other birds

Good Deed Of The Day

Learn about the importance of Zakat
and donate some money.

About islam

"But Allah would not punish
them while you, [O Muhammad],
are among them, and Allah
would not punish them while
they seek forgiveness."

Surah Anfal Verse 33

About Ramdan / Eid

We can remember Allah with
tongue or the heart or by both.
Following Allah's orders and
abstaining from His prohibitions
is also fasting.

About our Prophet

The Prophet mohamed is a role model for
all mankind till the day of judgement.
Believers look at his Sunnahs and learn
how they can implement the teachings
of Prophet in their lives.

Dua

Glory is to You, Master of power,
of dominion, of majesty and
greatness.

An-Nasa'i: 1133

I am grateful for ....

....

Coloring Page

Good Deed Of The Day
DAY : 19

Help a sibling or friend with their homework.

About islam

"Whatever the Messenger has given you - take; and what he has forbidden you - refrain from. And fear Allah; indeed, Allah is severe in penalty."

Surah Al-Hashr: 59:7

About Ramdan / Eid

In Egypt, colorful lanterns are lit in celebration of Ramadan becoming one of the most symbolic and colorful ways of celebrating this month, those lanterns that are lit during the evening and night, called "fanous".

About our Prophet

Prophet Muhammad's father Abdullah son of Abdul-Muttalib ,was the best and most pious among the sons of Abdul-Muttalib and his most beloved. he died while Muhammad was still in his mother's womb.

Dua

O Allah, You are my Lord, none has the right to be worshipped except You, You created me and I am Your servant and I abide to Your covenant and promise as best I can, I take refuge in You from the evil of which I have committed. I acknowledge Your favour upon me and I acknowledge my sin, so forgive me, for verily none can forgive in except You.
Al-Bukhari 7:150

I am grateful for ....
....

Coloring Page

Good Deed Of The Day
DAY : 20

Learn a new Islamic tradition or celebration

About islam

"Indeed, to Allah belongs the dominion of the heavens and the earth; He gives life and causes death. And you have not besides Allah any protector or any helper."
Surah Tawbah Ayat 116

About Ramdan / Eid

Moroccan town criers mark dawn prayers every morning for neighborhood, called Nafar these men will walk through neighborhoods at dawn prayer to awaken families and let everyone know that prayer will begin soon.

About our Prophet

Muhammad's mother was Aminah, daughter of Wahab son of Abd Manaf, She was also a believer in Allah. When he was born she said: "As soon as I put my child on the ground he leaned with his hands on the ground, raised his head to the skies and looked at the horizons . Then a voice called out to me saying:'The best of mankind has been born,so name him Muhammad.'"

Dua

O, Allah, we have reached the evening, calling You to witness, and calling the carriers of Your Throne to witness,and Your angels, and all of Your creation, that You are Allah, none has the right to be worshipped but You, Alone, without a partner, and that Muhammad is Your slave and Your Messenger.
At-Tirmidhi: 3501

I am grateful for

Coloring Page

Good Deed Of The Day

Learn to write your name in Arabic.

About islam

"Go forth, whether light or heavy, and strive with your wealth and your lives in the cause of Allah . That is better for you, if you only knew."

Surah Taubah Ayat 41

About Ramdan / Eid

In Albania, many Muslims will begin and end the day of fasting with special ballads for Ramadan.Along with playing the lodra, a traditional drum , many will invite families and loved ones for iftar and break their fast with religious ballads.

About our Prophet

Muhammad was not even seven years old when his mother died. After his mother's death, his grandfather Abdul-Muttalib assumed his guardianship. he treated Muhammad with more care and attention than his other children.

Dua

O Allah, grant my body health, O Allah, grant my hearing health, O Allah, grant my sight health. None has the right to be worshipped except You.O Allah,I take refuge with You from disbelief and poverty, and I take refuge with You from the punishment of the grave. None has the right to be worshipped except You.

Abu Dawud 4:324

I am grateful for ....
....

Coloring Page

Good Deed Of The Day

Collect donations for an Islamic charity.

About islam

"Unquestionably, to Allah belongs whatever is in the heavens and the earth. Unquestionably, the promise of Allah is truth, but most of them do not know"
Surah Yunus Ayat 55

About Ramdan / Eid

Beautiful act of worship and good deeds, Muslims in Cameroon will make it a practice of opening their doors right before iftar time, and invite anyone from outside who need to find somewhere to break their fast.

About our Prophet

Muhammad grew up to become a fine young man. He became known for his excellent manners, and because of the honesty in his conduct and dealings he was referred to as al- Sadiq (The Truthful One) and al-Amin (The Trustworthy One).

Dua

Allah is Sufficient for me, none has the right to be worshipped except Him, upon Him I rely and He is Lord of the exalted throne.

Abu Dawud 4:321

I am grateful for ....
....

Coloring Page

Good Deed Of The Day

Attend a lecture or seminar on Islam

About islam

"And if We give man a taste of mercy from Us and then We withdraw it from him, indeed, he is despairing and ungrateful.

Surah Hud Ayat 9-10

About Ramdan / Eid

Drummers will announce suhoor in Turkey, it's a tradition from Ottoman times, many neighborhoods across Turkey will have an appointed drummer, dressed in traditional Ottoman clothes.

About our Prophet

Muhammad worked as a trader between the cities of Mecca and Damascus, and earned a great reputation in the process. Having heard of the reputation of Muhammad, Lady Khadijah, one of the noblest of the Quraysh, commissioned him to take charge of some of her trading business between the two cities.

Dua

Glory is to You, O Allah, and praise is to You. I bear witness that there is none worthy of worship but You. I seek Your forgiveness and repent to You.

Abu Dawud: 4859

I am grateful for..
....

Ramdan word search solve the puzzle

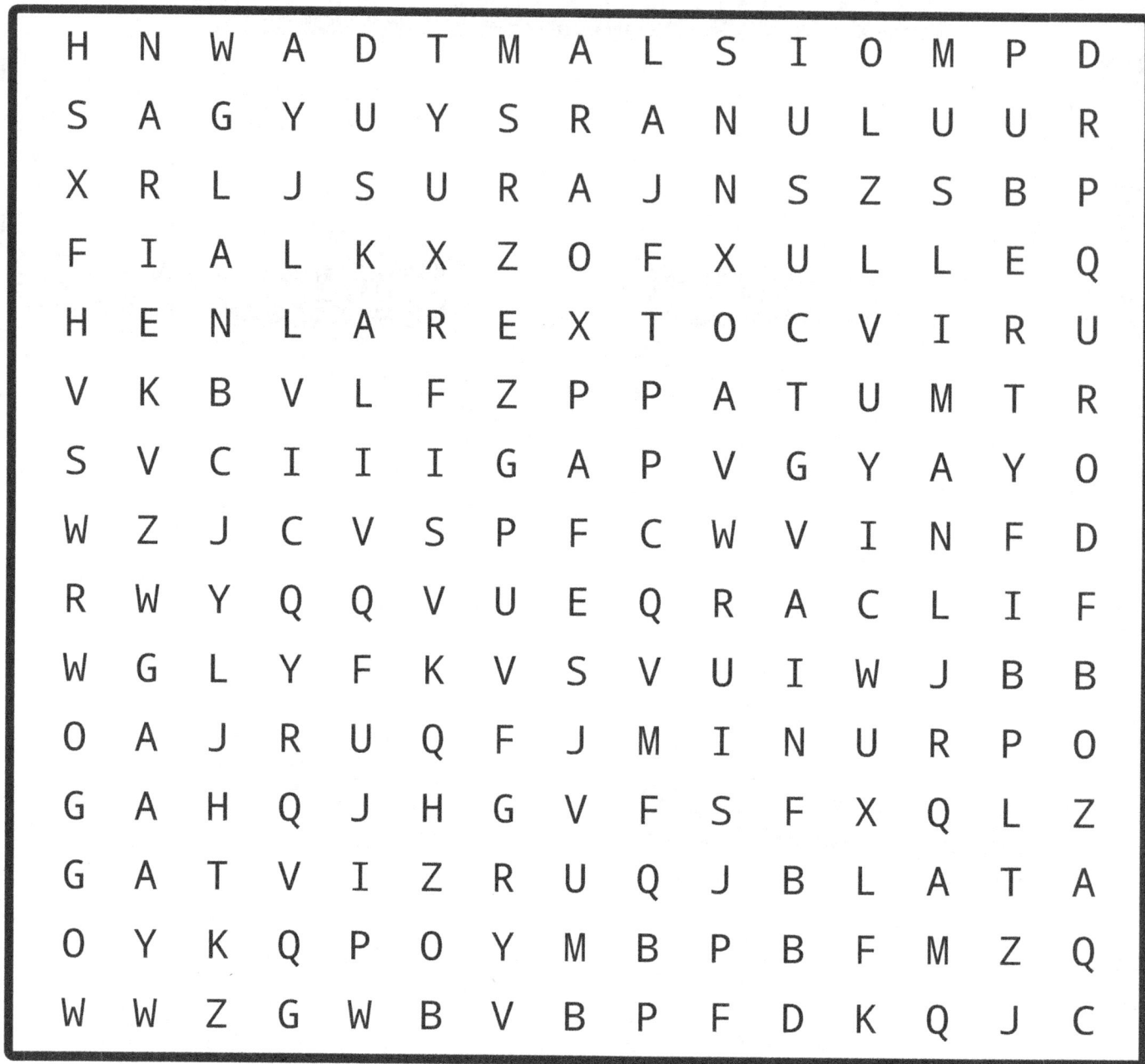

```
H N W A D T M A L S I O M P D
S A G Y U Y S R A N U L U U R
X R L J S U R A J N S Z S B P
F I A L K X Z O F X U L L E Q
H E N L A R E X T O C V I R U
V K B V L F Z P P A T U M T R
S V C I I I G A P V G Y A Y O
W Z J C V S P F C W V I N F D
R W Y Q Q V U E Q R A C L I F
W G L Y F K V S V U I W J B B
O A J R U Q F J M I N U R P O
G A H Q J H G V F S F X Q L Z
G A T V I Z R U Q J B L A T A
O Y K Q P O Y M B P B F M Z Q
W W Z G W B V B P F D K Q J C
```

ALLAH

DAWN

DUSK

FAST

FIVE PILLARS

ISLAM

LUNAR

MUSLIM

OBLIGATORY

PUBERTY

Good Deed Of The Day

Make a list of things to be thankful for and share it with your family.

About islam

my success is not but through Allah. Upon him I have relied, and to Him I return."

Surah Hud Ayat 88

About Ramdan / Eid

Moon Watchers,will mark Eid-al-Fitr in South Africa In a beautifully unique tradition, moon watchers or "maan kykers" in Afrikaans, will stand atop Signal Hill, the shore at the Sea Point Promenade,or at Three Anchor Bay and declare when Eid-al-Fitr

About our Prophet

His only daughter was Fatimah, who married Ali son of Abu Talib, and bore him Hasan and Husayn,Zaynab and Umm Kulthum, and another son who was named Mohsin by the Prophet before his birth.

Dua

I take refuge in Allah's perfect words from the evil He has created.

Ahmad 2:290, At-Tirmidhi 3:187

I am grateful for ....
....

Ramdan word search solve the puzzle

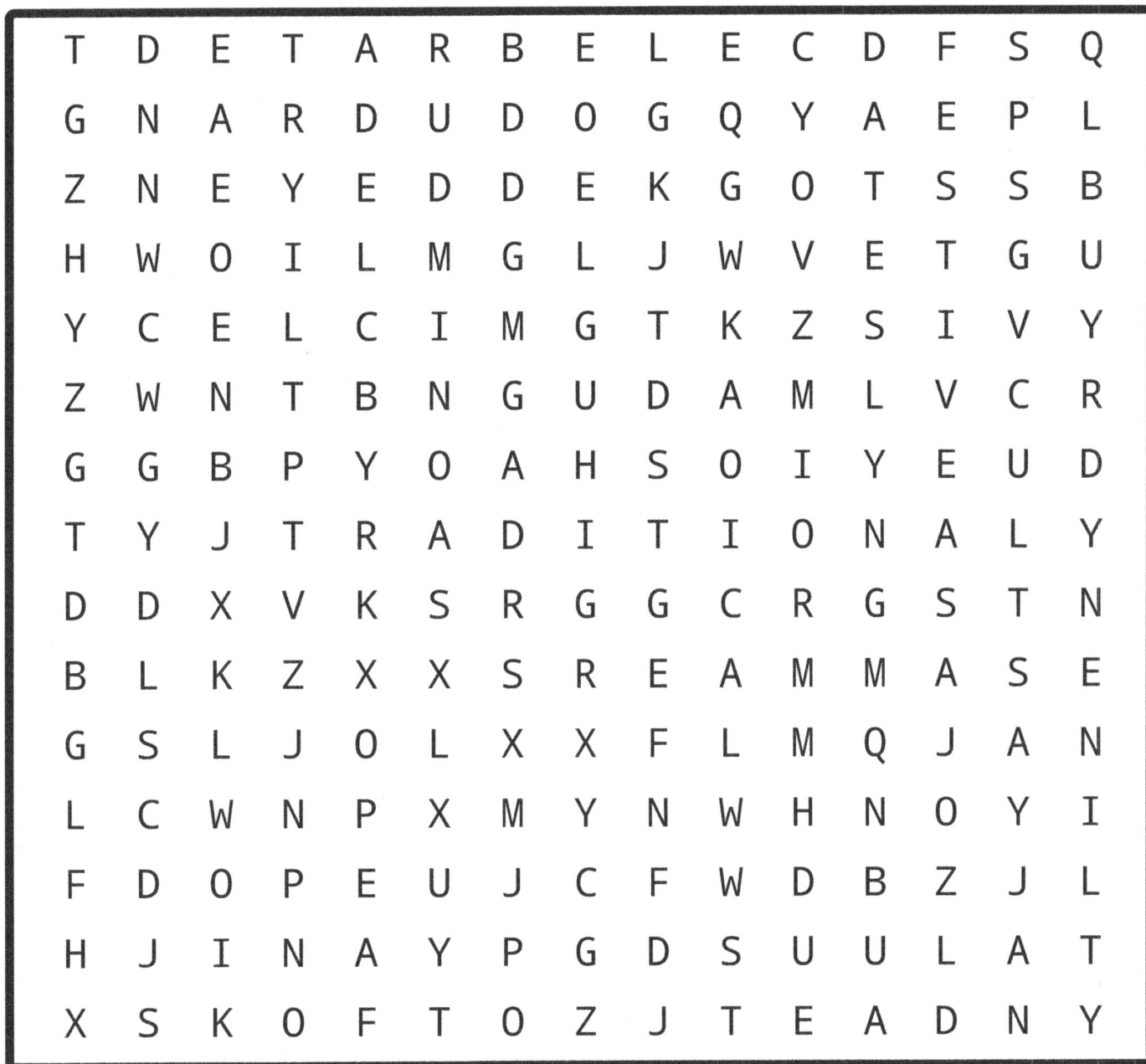

```
T  D  E  T  A  R  B  E  L  E  C  D  F  S  Q
G  N  A  R  D  U  D  O  G  Q  Y  A  E  P  L
Z  N  E  Y  E  D  D  E  K  G  O  T  S  S  B
H  W  O  I  L  M  G  L  J  W  V  E  T  G  U
Y  C  E  L  C  I  M  G  T  K  Z  S  I  V  Y
Z  W  N  T  B  N  G  U  D  A  M  L  V  C  R
G  G  B  P  Y  O  A  H  S  O  I  Y  E  U  D
T  Y  J  T  R  A  D  I  T  I  O  N  A  L  Y
D  D  X  V  K  S  R  G  G  C  R  G  S  T  N
B  L  K  Z  X  X  S  R  E  A  M  M  A  S  E
G  S  L  J  O  L  X  X  F  L  M  Q  J  A  N
L  C  W  N  P  X  M  Y  N  W  H  N  O  Y  I
F  D  O  P  E  U  J  C  F  W  D  B  Z  J  L
H  J  I  N  A  Y  P  G  D  S  U  U  L  A  T
X  S  K  O  F  T  O  Z  J  T  E  A  D  N  Y
```

ANCIENT   DUA   SUMMER
CELEBRATED   FESTIVE   TRADITIONAL
DATES   GOD
DAYLIGHT   OBLONG

Good Deed Of The Day

Holding doors open for others, and complimenting someone, can brighten someone's day

About islam

"There was certainly in their stories a lesson for those of understanding. Never was the Qur'an a narration invented, but a confirmation of what was before it and a detailed explanation of all things and guidance and mercy for a people who believe."
surah Yusuf Ayat 111

About Ramdan / Eid

Ramadan. It's a short but beautiful a blessed month; a month in which is a night better than a thousand months; a month in which Allah has made it compulsory upon you to fast by day and voluntary to pray by night

About our Prophet

Khadijah was thus the first woman to believe in the Messenger of Allah and the first woman to pray with him. She supported him wholeheartedly and spent all her wealth in the way of Allah. She was the first woman that the Prophet married.

Dua

I am pleased with Allah as a Lord, and Islam as a religion and Muhammad peace be upon to him as a Prophet.
Abu Dawud 4:318

I am grateful for ....
....

Ramdan word search solve the puzzle

```
H F A N O U S R T I F I B W B
A T H O L Y D A Y Q I H F E T
F D I E R A H S D B V J L U E
S A L A A M B W E A E H L Q S
W E H S F N Z B C V J S F A P
R E M E M B R A N C E J M N O
U Z A H R O B U F H D R A P I
T O Y M Z G K N M K A K Y S T
N L T E Z Z C M Z E B I C R Z
L T V P F K U K V E Z R Y P Z
O F P C J H V A U G Y M C O N
I T E Z H W M L F O V X U V F
O K Q R I U G Z Y N A R W U B
Y S G J S Z Z D Y O Y T L V A
G Z D A I W Z S H G R Y D Q A
```

FAITH	HOLYDAY	SHARE
FANOUS	REMEMBRANCE	SUFI
FITR	SAJJADA	
FIVE	SALAAM	

Good Deed Of The Day

Acts of kindness, such as saying please and thank you

About islam

"Indeed, Allah will not change the condition of a people until they change what is in themselves."
surah al Rad ayat 11

About Ramdan / Eid

Ramadan is the holiest month for all Muslims and Laylat Al Qadr is the holiest night .This night is so important that the Quran dedicates a special Surah to it.
Surah Al-Qadr (97).

About our Prophet

Prophet observed Laylat Al Qadr Praying on this night is also a Sunnah of our beloved Prophet . Messenger of Allah would engage himself in devotion during the last ten nights of Ramadan more than he did in any other time of the year.

Dua

O Allah, You are Forgiving and love forgiveness, so forgive me.

Ibn Majah: 3850

I am grateful for ....
....

Laylat Al Qadr

Laylat al Qadr is an Arabic world it means Night of Decree in English. It is also known as Lailatul Qadar in different parts of the world.

it's the holiest night in Ramadan which signifies its importance .

As mentioned in the sunnah, this night is better than a thousand months and worshiping on it is better than eighty-three years of worship.

That encourage Muslims to spend this night in worshipping, seeking forgiveness and asking Allah for his blessings in this world and hereafter.

Prophet Mohammad has Encourage the believers to seek Laylat Al Qadr during last 10 days of Ramadan.

Ramdan word search solve the puzzle

```
H T C Y T U D F A Z W H K T P
T F O K B Z U O T C E Q Y F H
O C M E K S Y R B U C T F R Y
G S M O S S T T T Q T E F A U
A I U O U H N U D T M P M H H
X D N O W Y J N G W Z C N O N
E K I T I Y A A F A I P N D S
C T T L S G C T E L M H G Y R
O B Y T O E I E J E C P M R L
Y L K S I H I L B M V I S R E
H T E G O T S L E G G X M P C
H D T D A H R Z O R Q B H L T
I H D R G O G G X H F E X N S
X K I U K W L T J O D G E M U
H D K R H I C U J W O H O
```

27TH   HOLIDAY   TOGETHER
COMMUNITY   HOLIEST NIGHT
DUTY   MECCA
FORTUNATE   RELIGIOUS

Good Deed Of The Day

Protect the environment by recycling, and picking up litter in the neighborhood.

About islam

"Our Lord, forgive me and my parents and the believers the Day the account is established." surah ibrahim Ayat 41

About Ramdan / Eid

Allah wishes us to be as spiritually clean as possible in the month of Ramadan so we can make the most of the month. You may seek forgiveness in your own fashion

About our Prophet

Through his teachings, the Messenger of Allah brought about harmony and peace between the different rivalries and warring groups and tribes of the city Madina and its surroundings. Whereas prior to his arrival, greed, enmity and wars prevailed between the inhabitants.

Dua

O Allah, I take refuge with You lest I should stray or be led astray, or slip or be tripped, or oppress or be oppressed, or behave foolishly or be treated foolishly.' slip: i.e. to commit a sin unintentionally.

Tirmidhi: 3426

I am grateful for

Coloring Page

Good Deed Of The Day

Donate gently used toys, clothes, and books to local charities

About islam

"Assuredly, Allah knows what they conceal and what they declare. Indeed, He does not like the arrogant."
Surah an Nahl ayat 23

About Ramdan / Eid

If you have any charitable projects in mind, now is the time to start planning them. Charity doesn't have to be monetary either.
The Prophet has said even smiling is charity. Why not make an attempt to rekindle lost relationships and mend ties.

About our Prophet

When his people didn't believe him, Jibreel (the Archangel) came to him and said, " Allah Almighty heard the allegations of your people and He asked the angel of the mountains to obey you. The angel of the mountains called Prophet Muhammad and said, " Ask me and I'll crush them. " Yet, Prophet Muhammad said, " No, I hope that Almighty will bring out of their seed people who worship him alone with no associates.

Dua

I seek Your pardon. Praise be to Allah who removed from me discomfort and gave me relief.
Ibnu Majah 26

I am grateful for..
....

Good Deed Of The Day

Show respect to others by listening when someone is talking, using kind words,

About islam

"On the Day when every soul will come disputing for itself, and every soul will be fully compensated for what it did, and they will not be wronged." Surah Nahl Ayat 111

About Ramdan / Eid

Getting into the habit of regularly conversing with God through dua helps us build a relationship with Him. You may say any dua you wish and in the language of your choice.

About our Prophet

Prophet Muhammad said, "I start the prayers, intending to lengthen them . I then hear a child crying so I make them shorter, knowing how emotional a child's mother gets."

Dua

O My Lord, Increase me in knowledge Sura Ta'ha, Ayat 114

I am grateful for ....
....

Good Deed Of The Day

Day : 30

Small acts of kindness and generosity can make a big difference in the world

About islam

"And do not walk upon the earth exultantly. Indeed, you will never tear the earth [apart], and you will never reach the mountains in height."
Surah Isra Ayat 37 Ayat 46

About Ramdan / Eid

After Ramadan, Muslims celebrate a three-day holiday called Eid-ul-Fitr. After this Eid , Muslims pray the holiday prayer in congregation in the morning, visit family and friends, and celebrate over food, gifts and activities for children.

About our Prophet

From his mercy is(peace and blessing be upon him) misprision from walking along with a widow or with a needy person and fulfill their requirements. He used to visit feeble and sick Muslims and attend their burials. He used to treat orphans effortlessly and charitably.

Dua

Oh Allah! Give to us in the world that which is good and in the hereafter that which is good, and save us from the torment of the Fire.
Bukhari and Muslim

I am grateful for ....
....

Eid al-Fitr

Salat al-Eid al-Fitr is a special prayer performed by Muslims on the morning of Eid al-Fitr, which marks the end of the holy month of Ramadan. It is typically performed in large congregations, either in mosques or in public spaces, such as parks or community centers.

The prayer consists of two rak'ahs (units of prayer) and includes additional takbirs (the phrase "Allahu Akbar" meaning "God is great") before and after the prayer.

The Imam (prayer leader) delivers a khutbah (sermon) after the prayer, which typically includes messages of gratitude, forgiveness, and brotherhood.

Salat al-Eid al-Fitr is an important part of Eid celebrations and is a means of expressing gratitude to Allah for the blessings of Ramadan and seeking His forgiveness for any wrongs committed during the month. It is also an opportunity for Muslims to come together .

Eid Mubarak

Made in the USA
Las Vegas, NV
24 March 2023

69629144R00059